On the Other Side of Through: Life After Loss

By

Angie Green

Published by

Queen V Publishing
Dayton, OH
QueenVPublishing.com

Queen V Publishing
Dayton, OH
QueenVPublishing.com

Copyright © 2018 by Angie Green

All rights reserved. No part of this book may be reproduced or transmitted in any form or by any means, electronic or mechanical, without prior written consent of the author, except for the inclusion of brief quotes in a review.

Unless otherwise noted, Scriptures were taken from the King James Version of the Holy Bible.

Library of Congress Control Number: 2018934033

ISBN-13: 978-0-9962991-1-4

Cover design by Charlotte L. Jenkins of 31 Woman
Edited by Valerie J. Lewis Coleman of Pen of the Writer and Tenita C. Johnson of So It Is Written

Printed in the United States of America

Acknowledgements

I thank my Lord and Savior, Jesus Christ, for giving me courage and ability to write my story. Thank You, for the gifts of grace and mercy. Because of who You are, I will forever give You praise.

To my husband, Jonathan: Since the beginning of our relationship, you've been a loving, caring man. Through the rough patches, we grew to respect and love each other even more. I know that God has a plan for us that is bigger than what we can see or imagine.

To my mother, Alberta Richardson: Thank you for praying me through my trials and encouraging me to pray and lean on God.

To my dad, George Washington: Thank you for being a great father. I wish you were here to have one of our good talks. I'd give anything to hear you say, "I'm proud of you, baby." I miss you, Daddy!

To my beautiful children, Raven Olivia and Justin B.: I couldn't have asked for better children. You motivate me to excel and you're so helpful to me. Thank you for encouraging me to write this book. Mommy loves you!

To my sister, Elizabeth (Liz) Richardson: Thanks for praying with—and for—me. You are a great big sister.

To my cousin, Evelyn Carter: Thanks for checking on me and encouraging me to keep going. Your endless support has not gone unnoticed.

To my awesome spiritual parents and pastors, Bishop Don W. Shelby and Lady Bonita Shelby: Thank you for your continual prayers and encouragement. I appreciate that when you haven't see me for a while, you call or text to see if I'm okay.

To my family, friends and spiritual family at Burning Bush International Ministries: Thank you for helping me through hard times, offering words of encouragement and many acts of kindness.

Dedication

I dedicate this book to my baby girl, JóNiah B. Green. I often dream about you. I think about you growing up, dancing, enjoying life. I miss the wonderful hugs you gave me every day. I love you!

Table of Contents

Foreword 11
Introduction 13
JóNiah 15
In the Beginning 21
A Mother's Worst Fear 23
My Stages of Grief 29
    Bargaining 31
    Denial 33
    Anger 37
    Depression 41
    Acceptance 45
My Faith & Trust 51
    Tested 53
    Trusting God in Grief 57
    Scriptures on Trusting God 59
    Quotes on Trusting God 63
    Scriptures for Comfort 67
As I Grieved 71
    He Needed His Wife 73

They Needed Their Mother 77
What Not to Say to a Grieving Person 81
In Memory of JóNiah 83
Resources for Grief 85
Want to Experience More? 87
About Angie Green 89
About Queen V Publishing 91

On the Other Side of Through

Foreword

Millions of people die in the United States every year: expectedly and unexpected. Loss is a normal part of life.

As a social worker, I support individuals with grief, loss and end-of-life issues. But what happens when the professional becomes the griever? I found myself in a strange situation when I had to request the support of another professional to help my family through traumatic events.

On the Other Side of Through is a life-changing testament to the power of prayer and its use as a coping mechanism. This book provided clarity and healing for a family that has dealt with layers of tragedies. Angie Green is a warrior who triumphantly utilized her spiritual faith to take her through many of life's storms.

> *To everything there is a season, a time for every purpose under heaven: a time to weep, and a time to laugh; a time to mourn, and a time to dance.*
> —Ecclesiastes 3:1, 4

Many Bible stories demonstrate how God comforts His people in times of sorrow. Job cleaved frantically to God despite catastrophic loss and unhelpful friends. David, "a man after God's own heart," openly grieved the death of his son. And a modern mother, who grieves the loss of multiple children, was also comforted by God's love.

I am proud to know Angie on personal and professional levels. I have adopted *On the Other Side of Through* into my therapeutic catalog as a resource to clients experiencing grief and loss.

Elizabeth R. Richardson, licensed social worker
MA, LMSW

On the Other Side of Through

Introduction

The death of a child violates the natural order of life.

Writing this book was therapeutic for me. Although reliving the tragedy was difficult, composing helped me process through my emotions. No longer willing to suffer in silence, I leveraged my pain to help others grieving loved ones. By transparently sharing my experience, I was free to express my reliance on God.

Reflection questions are provided throughout the book. Meditate, allow yourself to experience your emotions and then journal your thoughts. The process helped me better navigate my grief and I hope it serves you to do the same.

My prayer is that this book helps you learn how to accept the death of your dear loved one, stand firm in your faith and let God get you to the other side of through.

Angie Green

Angie Green

On the Other Side of Through

JóNiah

We were ecstatic the day we found out we were expecting again.

Our daughter was born after the Michigan blackout on August 27, 2003. She weighed six pounds, six ounces. Her brown complexion, black curly hair and big brown eyes won our hearts on sight.

Although we knew our blessing-to-be was a girl, we had not chosen a name for her. We took the first three letters of Jonathan (my husband's name), added "iah" and then declared the "o" silent to create JóNiah (pronounced ja-nī-yah).

JóNiah was a smart baby. She took her first steps at ten months old. She was my inquisitive; daredevil who loved trying things that other kids were too afraid to do.

As JóNiah got older, she danced around the house like a ballerina. So, when she was four, I enrolled her in dance school. She cried at almost every lesson—I think she preferred to dance to her own rhythm—so we ended the sessions.

That same year, she started preschool. Since I was a stay-at-home mom, JóNiah hadn't been around many children. Although things started roughly, she acclimated to the other children. Once she managed the challenges of preschool, she was a joy to her teachers and peers. She loved counting and reading.

At seven years old, we revisited her taking dance lessons and re-enrolled her in ballet class. After just two sessions, she wanted to try tap dance and hip-hop jazz. She excelled at all three.

JóNiah—who had her daddy wrapped around all her fingers and toes—had such a sweet spirit. She could do no wrong by him as his princess. Whenever JóNiah wanted something, she asked her father first. She knew he'd agree to whatever she wanted.

In June 2012, JóNiah completed the third grade with a 3.8 GPA. The following month, she performed at her first dance recital and received medals for her performances. We hosted a reception for family and friends to celebrate her accomplishments. We were so proud of our baby girl.

JóNiah was such a graceful, dainty young lady who did everything with perfection. She took pride in her appearance. Her clothes and hair—which she loved to wear in braids or a ponytail—were always in place. She tried to incorporate her favorite color, purple, into her daily ensemble.

If she got a tiny spot on her clothes, she ran to change them. If the blemish was bad, she took a bath. JóNiah, my girly girl, wore lots of lip gloss.

Late spring of the same year, I took the kids shopping for summer clothes. Raven and Justin, JóNiah's older and younger siblings, respectively, liked the clothes I chose for them. JóNiah, on the other hand, not so much. She dared to be different.

Because I didn't have her fashion savvy, she said, "Mom, don't be upset. I just want a certain look and Aunt Liz knows what I'm looking for."

This same aunt nicknamed her niece "Niah B" (short for JóNiah Brenaè) when she was four.

On Saturday, July 21, 2012, I prepared for work and instructed JóNiah to get her bag together for her friend's overnight pool party. I left the kids home with their father who had been on the road working for three weeks. They were excited to spend quality time with him.

When I returned home, I checked JóNiah's bag to make sure she had everything she needed for the hotel sleepover. We had never allowed the children to spend the night anywhere without us, but JóNiah charmed her father into agreeing. She was mature for her age and knew how to act in public, but since this sleepover was her first, we clarified our expectations.

Her father said, "You behave, have fun and be careful."

We finalized the logistics for the weekend. On Saturday, I would drop off JóNiah to the sleepover, take Justin on a playdate and then pick up JóNiah Sunday morning in time for youth service at our church. She looked forward to attending because it was the youth conference. She was excited to see her friends and to learn more about God.

While on the play date, I got a call from a detective.

"Mrs. Green." He paused. "There's been an accident. You need to get to St. Mary Hospital right away."

Anxious; I scurried to gather Justin and then rushed to the hospital. When I arrived at the emergency room, the detective tried to explain what happened. I pushed past him to the room where a swarm of doctors surrounded my baby. They intubated her, performed chest compressions and worked to resuscitate my once vibrant child with oxygen.

My husband sat in the corner with tears of disbelief pooling in his eyes.

I held JóNiah's hand, caressed her face, whispered, "Breathe, baby. Breathe." I wanted her to cry for me. I wanted her to make a noise. Any sign of movement would have given me a tittle of hope.

After about three minutes—which seemed like an eternity—they declared her dead.

"We have done all we can do for JóNiah."

She had drowned in the hotel swimming pool minutes after I left her there.

Grief consumed me. I screamed. "God, why did You let this happen to us again? Please don't take my baby! Please, Lord, I'm begging You! Don't take my baby!"

Two elders from our church came to the hospital to support us. Although they prayed and tried to encourage us, I felt my faith in God leave me.

Angie Green

On the Other Side of Through

In the Beginning

My most-proudest accomplishment is being a mother. I had my first baby, Raven Olivia, at sixteen years old. Despite the responsibilities of rearing a child as a child, I was—and still am—a great mother to her.

Seven years later, I met Jonathan and learned that we were expecting twin girls. At 23 weeks, complications led to premature delivery. One of our daughters was stillborn; the other lived for a few hours. Although I had only loved the girls in vitro, their death was traumatic. Jonathan and I grieved and then decided to move on from it.

We married the following year. Our family included two children: my eight-year-old daughter and his sixteen-year-old son, Jonathan, Junior.

Two years into our marriage, we found out that I was pregnant with a healthy baby girl. For months, we didn't tell anyone about the pregnancy in case we had complications like with the twins. In good health, I went full-term to deliver a healthy baby girl: JóNiah.

Fourteen months later, my sixteen-year-old stepson was killed in a car accident. We were flung from the bliss of newfound parenthood to intense grieving.

A few weeks after burying Jonathan, Jr., I learned that I was pregnant with a boy. With the trauma and chaos of losing a son, we battled between celebration and grief. We were thankful that God blessed us with another opportunity to rear a son.

Stress caused complications with the pregnancy, but I stayed prayerful and trusted that our son would be fine. Justin arrived six weeks early and spent eight days in the NICU. I didn't realize it at the time, but God was preparing me to remain prayerful and faithful in adversity.

On the Other Side of Through

A Mother's Worst Fear

Having to bury a child is unimaginable; a mother's worst fear. Having to bury four children is unfathomable.

I still believed God; however, my faith was tested beyond comprehension. I tried to figure out what I had done to upset God so. Why else would He take four of my babies? Obviously, He had it out for me. He wanted to punish me for not fully serving Him.

> "In our hearts, we all know that death is a part of life. In fact, death gives meaning to our existence because it reminds us how precious life is."
> — Anonymous

The Ultimate No for Help: Seeing a Therapist

My upbringing was spiritual. My family spent lots of time at church. Whenever someone was experiencing "trials and tribulations," my parents and grandparents said, "People don't need a therapist. They just need God."

We were taught to pray about everything; take your burdens to the altar and leave them there. If you experienced a loss, you could talk about it for a while. However, if you spoke on it too long, you were told, "Take it to God and let Him handle it."

As I matured, I learned that people process things differently. I asked God for guidance and He led me to seek professional help. He gave me permission to speak with a tangible, earthly being to work out my grief.

A therapist can shed light on things you may not have considered, help you process your feelings and provide productive coping mechanisms. Besides, what do you do when you are so overwhelmed with grief and anger that you don't want to talk to God?

Lord, How Much More?

Four years of trying to figure out this devastation on my own, I sought professional help. I researched the internet for a Christian therapist who specialized in the type of grief that I was experiencing.

Before my first session with Dr. Matthews, I tried to come up with a reason to cancel. When I finally mustered the strength to go to her office, I was extremely nervous. I repeated in my mind, *I am not going to cry.*

As I talked about my feelings, the flood of emotions overwhelmed me. I cried uncontrollably. Once I regained my composure, I realized that a good cry was what I needed.

In only one hour, I left with a new outlook. I shared the experience with my husband and returned for more professional help.

I never openly expressed my feelings and I didn't "look like" a grieving mother; whatever that means. People close to me, including my family, didn't know that I was seeing a therapist. I didn't want to be told that therapists and counselors are for crazy people or that I needed to trust God more.

I learned so much during my therapy; especially understanding that not only was I grieving JóNiah, but I was grieving years of losses.

In addition to the death of four children, within a span of seven months, I lost two nephews — to whom I was very close — and my father. Loss on top of loss thrust me into an emotional crisis: depression.

Dr. Matthews encouraged me to meditate and take time for myself.

I resisted. "If I take time for me, who's taking care of my family?"

It felt selfish, until Dr. Matthews explained that I needed to take care of myself, if I wanted to be around for my family. She assured me, "They will be fine."

As I yielded to the process, I acquired techniques which helped me cope. When I get emotional or stressed, I meditate, write my feelings in a journal and pray. I spend time alone, treat myself to a spa visit or enjoy a movie.

As our sessions continued, I shared memories about JóNiah. My healing spilled over to the entire family as we created new traditions. We scheduled more quality family time and took turns speaking about our individual and collective memories of her.

Because of my first-hand, life-changing experience with therapy, I recommend it to anyone experiencing a life trauma. With guided professional help, I expanded my perspective in a non-biased way.

I was taught that Christians don't need a therapist to help with grief or loss. I believe in prayer and its life-changing effects. I also know that talking with a professional helped me. Had I not sought help from a therapist, I believe that I would still be stuck grieving; without an escape and uncertain about how to activate my faith.

Bereavement—to be deprived by death—has taken me through a whirlwind of emotions: denial, anger, guilt, abandonment.

At the time of this writing, JóNiah had been gone five years. I expected to be over the hard part of grieving, but I now understand that it takes time. Time without a due date. Time to comprehend the loss. Time to absorb how it affects you. Time to find a new normal. And when the loss is a child or parent, the effect is far greater.

You cannot place a time limit to your grieving. Some say that the pain eases after two years because you've had the opportunity to twice relive holidays, birthdays and other special occasions. Not my testimony.

An annoying interaction is the on-going inquiry about how I'm doing. When I tell someone that I'm having a hard time or still processing the loss, a common response is, "Oh, I thought you would be past that by now." Really? Not now…not ever.

Grief can hold you hostage and keep you stuck in multiple feelings. You don't know how to release the emotions to move forward. Much like an airplane in a holding pattern, I circled the runway of peace, but could not land on it.

I didn't graduate from one stage of grief to the next. Grief is not a chronological experience with a checklist of phases to complete. I have been woven into the tapestry of grief's stages like a massive loom: held under tension to facilitate the interweaving of God's plan.

According to medical professionals, grief has five to seven stages. I believe I experienced all of them at once. I bargained and pleaded, asking God to give me back my baby. I moved into denial and then anger. I felt like God had ignored me for several years. Every day, I battled to accept the unavoidable: JóNiah was never coming home.

My Stages of Grief

Angie Green

On the Other Side of Through

Bargaining

While the doctors worked to revive JóNiah, I tried to bargain with God.

"I know I haven't been living in my full potential, but please don't take my innocent baby girl. I promise to serve You more. I will pray four times a day and read my Bible more."

After trying to bargain and negotiate with God, I said, "Well, if I had done all those things, maybe I wouldn't be going through this now. God, take me instead. If You just want a soul, then it should be mine; not my baby's."

I cried. I bargained. I felt like I was losing the battle of fighting for my child's life and losing control of myself.

One day, while praying, God revealed that I didn't lose the battle. He was not punishing me.

Although I wanted what I wanted, I had not considered JóNiah's quality of life if doctors had been able to revive her. She was without oxygen for too long which caused brain damage. Her quality of life would have been diminished. God wasn't punishing me, He was saving JóNiah–and the family—from on-going suffering.

Yet today, when the pain seems too great, I bargain with God. Those times when it feels like she's been gone for years and only one day, I plead with Him.

Reflection Questions

Have you ever tried to bargain with God?

_____

If yes, for what did you bargain?

_____
_____
_____
_____
_____

Did you get the results you wanted?

_____
_____
_____
_____
_____

On the Other Side of Through

Denial

Once the doctors told me that I had lost yet another child, denial overtook me. I felt trapped in a nightmare and couldn't wake. I convinced myself that she was away and she'd be home soon.

In this stage, I found it more difficult to explain to my surviving children what happened to their sister. Raven was eighteen years old; Justin had just turned seven. Justin looked up to JóNiah; she was his best friend. How could I explain something to him that I didn't understand myself?

No one can tell you how to feel or how long you should feel it. Five years since we lost JóNiah, 13 years since we lost Jonathan, Jr. and 17 years since we laid Jaila and Jelene to rest and I still revert to denial. I forget that our children are no longer on Earth. If all our children were alive, they'd range in age from 12 to 29. With Raven off to college, I should still have four children at home, not just one.

For me, the denial stage was the worst because you hold out hope for a different outcome. Once denial wanes, you are slapped with the reality that you will never see your loved one alive again. The emotions and tears flare.

I have had several dreams where JóNiah was alive and well. Someone had taken her from us and we got her back years later. Every time I awake from that dream, it throws me back to square one: denial. I know that my baby girl is deceased and will not return, but denial plays tricks on my mind to believe she is still here.

I had lost all hope and faith in God, but eventually, I got back to praying and seeking Him for guidance. I asked Him to help me understand.

> *For My thoughts are not your thoughts, neither are your ways My ways, saith the Lord. For as the heavens are higher than the earth, so are My ways higher than your ways, and My thoughts than your thoughts.*
> —Isaiah 5:8-9

My sanity required an active prayer life and a committed relationship with God. Otherwise, I may have ended up in a psychiatric hospital, or at least I assume that would have been my fate. Burying four children is enough to drive one insane.

Reflection Questions

Have I been honest with others about my feelings?
_____

If not, why not? When will I start?
_____
_____
_____
_____
_____

If yes, how have I been honest about my feelings?
_____
_____
_____
_____
_____

Angie Green

Anger

I stayed angry at God for years. I couldn't understand how the forgiving, loving God allowed me to experience so many deaths; especially those of my children. The anger boiled inside me like an active volcano, but I didn't know how to release it.

I didn't want to go to church. God took my baby and I was mad about it. I would never see her graduate, marry, become a mother. I would never see her excel in dance or execute the perfect pirouette.

"Why did You take my healthy baby when children are suffering from abuse and neglect?"

JóNiah was blessed to have two loving parents in the home. Her future looked bright. Her life should have been spared. As selfish as it sounds, why didn't God take an abused child out of misery instead of my vibrant baby? My grief and hatred grew so strong that all I could do was blame God.

I was 23-weeks pregnant when the miscarriage took my twin daughters. I experienced sadness, heaviness and self-doubt. If I had been more careful and rested more, maybe I would have carried them to term. I couldn't get past my feelings from the miscarriage, but JóNiah's death brought a different type of agony. Was God punishing me for all the bad choices I had made? Was God telling me that I wasn't worthy to be a mother to that precious little girl? Had God left me to get through this trauma on my own? The devil whispered in my ear attempting to turn me against God. When you're weak, vulnerable and spiritually disconnected, the enemy can easily manipulate and deceive you.

Reflection Questions

Have I embraced my pain to release it?

_____

If not, why not? When will I start?

_____
_____
_____
_____

If yes, what steps have I taken to embrace my pain?

_____
_____
_____
_____
_____

Have I opened my heart to healing moments?

_____

If not, why not? When will I start?

_____
_____
_____
_____
_____

If yes, what steps have I taken toward opening my heart to healing moments?

_____

_____

_____

_____

_____

On the Other Side of Through

Depression

Depression is anger turned inward. I blamed myself for her drowning. If only I hadn't left when I did…. If I had stayed 30 minutes longer, an extra hour, she'd still be with me. Nothing anyone said or did made me think otherwise.

Satan subtly reminded me, "It was the first time you let your daughter spend the night and look what happened."

I dwelled on that thought until I hated myself. My actions caused this pain. Because of me, JóNiah's not here and my family is suffering. I stayed in a perpetual state of sadness and gloom. Worthless. Guilty. Abandoned.

Loss was not new to me. My grandmother and father died of long-term illness. Their absence was painful but expected.

The miscarriage was precluded by premature labor during the fourth month. Although extremely hard to accept, I had time to anticipate the outcome and my relationship with the twins was solely in vitro.

But JóNiah was different. She was young, vibrant and in our lives for eight years. I blamed myself and then I blamed God.

During my depression, I became very irritated. The smallest things triggered me. I snapped at people who tried to be nice. I cried until my eyes were swollen. I had intense headaches for days. Depression affected my sleep. I stayed tired and struggled to get up in the mornings. I was three years into my personal hell before I knew I was depressed.

My dysfunction got so bad that I couldn't get Justin ready for school. I sat in the showroom of my business, Elegant Events, and said, "I don't want to run this anymore." I considered selling the business and taking a financial loss. What harm could one more loss do? I lost myself and had to get a grip on my life.

During a Sunday service, my spiritual father prayed for people who were depressed. I focused on his words and the tears flowed. When he was done praying, a huge load lifted off me. I was consumed with emptiness as if I had just given birth to a full-term baby. That emptiness was the spirit of depression leaving me.

Slowly, but surely, my family got stronger in the Word.

Reflection Questions

Have I given myself permission to grieve freely, at my own pace and in ways that best suit me?

_____

If not, why not? When will I start?

_____
_____
_____
_____
_____

If yes, in what ways have I grieved?

_____
_____
_____
_____
_____

Have I allowed for moments of happiness without guilt?

_____

If not, why not? When will I start?

_____

_____

_____

_____

_____

If yes, how have I allowed for guiltless moments of happiness?

_____

_____

_____

_____

On the Other Side of Through

Acceptance

Instead of accepting JóNiah's death, for four years, I pretended that she was far away, and I just couldn't get to her. Denial.

Now that I have reached a place of acceptance, people assume that I am over losing her. Quite the opposite. My acceptance does not mean I'm over the loss. Acceptance is my choice to live as best as possible without her. I accept that she's not physically here with me, but I am far from being over her death. I have learned—and continue to learn—how to keep living. In the rough times, I reminisce on the wonderful memories we created.

We had to adjust. We had no choice but to reorganize our lives to exclude her. We hadn't realized how different things would be, until school started.

We had a morning routine to get Raven off to college and JóNiah and Justin ready for grade school. The transition was difficult, especially for Justin.

He admired his sister and best friend. She walked him to his class in the morning and met him there in the afternoon. When he needed help, he asked her first. If I cooked a meal that Justin, my picky-eater, didn't like, JóNiah encouraged him to at least try it.

Instead of having his big sister to help him tie his shoes, play tag or hug him when he was upset, he was alone.

Through my grieving, I realized that acceptance required me to forgive myself and others. I fought against forgiveness. I wanted to hold onto the hurt, pain and guilt as if it kept JóNiah close to me. Once I moved past the internal war and allowed forgiveness to win, the battle of acceptance began.

Every time we tried to move forward, it felt like we were leaving JóNiah; forgetting her. But with prayer, family counseling, quality time and sharing happy memories of JóNiah, we learned that we were not forgetting her.

Years later, we are still at the beginning of accepting her absence. I am so thankful for technology! If I want to hear her voice or see her face, I watch videos of her.

Reflection Questions

Have I given myself permission to fully experience love for my loved one?

_____

If not, why not? When will I start?

_____

_____

_____

_____

If yes, in what ways have I given myself permission to experience love for my loved one?

_____

_____

_____

_____

Have I honored my loved one in ways I choose?

_____

If not, why not? When will I start?

_____

_____

_____

_____

_____

If yes, in what ways have I honored my loved one?

_____

_____

_____

_____

_____

Have I started to live in the aftermath of the death of my loved one?

_____

If not, why not? When will I start?

_____

_____

_____

_____

If yes, what steps have I taken toward living in the aftermath?

_____

_____

_____

_____

_____

Angie Green

My Faith & Trust

Angie Green

On the Other Side of Through

Tested

> While some things come to test your faith, others come to destroy it.

God was punishing me. Some people who don't give God a thought have never experienced the death of a child. It's unfair and frustrating.

Because she died the month before her birthday, I become incapacitated in July and August. Dysfunctional, debilitated, drained.

Likewise, my relationship with God changed. Although my faith carried me through this tragedy, the hurt remained. The thought of losing my faith can be mind-boggling.

> "When I lose my faith, I lose my confidence. I lose my courage. That's when I give up."
> — Bishop Don W. Shelby Jr.

Giving up is not an option. I will keep fighting, not despite JóNiah, but because of her.

Two months before JóNiah died, I heard a sermon based on Matthew 17:20 entitled *Faith: Things are Subject to Change*.

And Jesus said unto them, Because of your unbelief: for verily I say unto you, If ye have faith as a grain of mustard seed, ye shall say unto this mountain, Remove hence to yonder place; and it shall remove; and nothing shall be impossible unto you.
—Matthew 17:20

    I wasn't ready. While my faith was tested, I felt like God had abandoned me. He left me to deal with JóNiah's death on my own. In my heart, I knew He was there, but grief overshadowed His presence. I felt alone; isolated.

    I struggled to attend church because I harbored anger toward God for allowing this life disruption. I didn't want to answer any more questions about how I felt. I wasn't ready to be around little girls who reminded me of JóNiah.

    Raised in the church, believing God at His Word was the cornerstone principle of my faith. God had not left me to handle this all-consuming grief alone. Like the poem, *Footsteps in the Sand*, He carried me. But, loneliness wouldn't leave me alone.

    God had to be testing my faith. I had to remember that God is all-knowing (omniscient), all-present (omnipresent) and all-powerful (omnipotent). I had to reflect on how He must have felt when His Son was murdered on the cross.

I had to rely on God to get to my next level. I needed Him to keep my sanity. I needed Him to function day-to-day. My faith kept me from shriveling up in a corner to die.

I still grieve. I'm still angry. I still believe God is with me. Whenever I get the urge to cry, I cry so the healing can do what it needs to do. God is preparing me for greater things, so I must process through the grief to get to the other side.

When I finally surrendered my will to Him, He positioned me to minister to others. Even if they lost faith in Him, I serve them to find it and show them how to release the hurt and pain. By sharing my story, others are comforted knowing that calm follows the storm. When I hear that someone is enduring a similar situation, I pray for them. I never desired to be a published author, but God is turning my tragedy into His triumph. God is using me.

Angie Green

On the Other Side of Through

Trusting God in Grief

Somewhere along this journey, my shattered faith affected my trust. So, once I accepted that my life would never be the same, I had to learn to trust God again. I had to trust that He was with me. I had to trust that He would bring me through the grief and pain. I had to trust that He had a plan for my new life.

Trusting and leaning on God was my only hope. It was my only way out of grief.

People often ask me how I manage to smile when I've buried four children.

"Faith. I learned to trust and depend on God through — and on the other side of — my grief."

Initially, I felt defeated, but I knew that feeling was temporary. How? Because He had already proven Himself.

> *By whom also we have access by faith into this grace wherein we stand, and rejoice in hope of the glory of God. And not only so, but we glory in tribulations also: knowing that tribulation worketh patience; And patience, experience; and experience, hope:*
> —Romans 5:2-5

Angie Green

On the Other Side of Through

Scriptures on Trusting God

I process through my grief by reading, speaking and meditating on Scriptures. One of my favorite Scriptures reminds me that if I simply trust Him, He will shield and protect me. It reminds me that He's with me through the process.

> *The God of my rock: in Him will I trust; He is my shield, and the horn of my salvation, my high tower, and my refuge, my savior; Thou savest me from violence.*
> —2 Samuel 22:3

> *As for God, His way is perfect; the Word of the Lord is tried; He is a buckler to all them that trust in Him.*
> —2 Samuel 22:31

> *Ye that fear the Lord, trust in the Lord: He is their help and their shield.*
> —Psalm 115:11

Trust in the Lord with all your heart; lean not unto thine own understanding. In all thy ways acknowledge Him and He shall direct thy paths.
—Proverbs 3:5-6

"For I know the thoughts that I think toward you," saith the Lord, "thoughts of peace and not of evil, to give you an expected end."
—Jeremiah 29:11

Blessed are they that mourn; for they shall be comforted.
—Matthew 5:4

Jesus answered and said unto them, "Verily I say unto you, if ye have faith, and doubt not, ye shall not only do this which is done to the fig tree, but also if ye shall say unto this mountain, be thou removed, and be thou cast into the sea; it shall be done."
—Matthew 21:21

And He said unto me, "My grace is sufficient for thee: for My strength is made perfect in weakness." Most gladly therefore will I rather glory in my infirmities, that the power of Christ may rest upon me.
—2 Corinthians 12:9

Casting all your care upon Him; for He careth for you.
—1 Peter 5:7

Reflection Questions

What Scriptures remind you to trust God especially in the storm?

_____
_____
_____
_____
_____
_____
_____
_____
_____

Angie Green

On the Other Side of Through

Quotes on Trusting God

[1] "Faith is taking the first step even when you don't see the whole staircase."
—Martin Luther King, Jr.

"Faith isn't the ability to believe long and far into the misty future. It's simply taking God at His Word and taking the next step."
—Joni Erickson Tada

"To live by faith means to make decisions based on what God says, even though you do not yet see the results."
—Tony Evans

"Faith is believing that God is going to take you places before you even get there."
—Matthew Barnett

"Pray, and let God worry."
—Martin Luther

---

[1] Source: *Trusting God Sayings and Quotes,* online: www.WiseOldSayings.com/Trusting-God-Quotes (accessed January 19, 2018).

"Never be afraid to trust an unknown future to a known God."
—Corrie ten Boom

"It is good to remind ourselves that the will of God comes from the heart of God and that we need not be afraid."
—Warren Wiersbe

"Faith is not just about being faithful; it's also about trusting in God's faithfulness."
—John D. Barry

"Worry implies that we don't quite trust that God is big enough, powerful enough or loving enough to take care of what's happening in our lives."
—Francis Chan

"Faith is accepting that you don't know, and trusting that God does."
—Brandi Keeler

"God's promises are like the stars; the darker the night, the brighter they shine."
—David Nicholas

"Grieving is a necessary passage and difficult transition to finally letting go of sorrow. It is not a permanent rest stop."
—Dodinsky

"Some people come into our lives and quickly go. Some stay for a while and leave footprints on our hearts and we are never, ever the same."
—C.C. Scott

"Whatever you're facing today, keep going. Keep moving. Keep hoping. Keep pressing. There's victory on the other side!"
—Mandy Hale

"You can do the IMPOSSIBLE because you have been through the UNIMAGINABLE."
—Christina Rasmussen

"Grief is not a disorder, a disease or a sign of weakness. It is an emotional, physical and spiritual necessity, the price you pay for love. The only cure for grief is to grieve."
—Earl Grollman

"The darker the night, the brighter the stars. The deeper the grief, the closer is God!"
—Fyodor Dostoyevsky

Angie Green

On the Other Side of Through

Scriptures for Comfort

For His anger endureth but a moment; in His favor is life: weeping may endure for a night, but joy cometh in the morning.
—Psalms 30:5

He healeth the broken in heart, and bindeth up their wounds.
—Psalms 147:3

Verily, verily, I say unto you, That ye shall weep and lament, but the world shall rejoice: and ye shall be sorrowful, but your sorrow shall be turned into joy.
—John 16:20

Blessed be God, even the Father of our Lord Jesus Christ, the Father of mercies, and the God of all comfort; Who comforteth us in all our tribulation, that we may be able to comfort them which are in any trouble, by the comfort wherewith we ourselves are comforted of God.
—2 Corinthians 1:3-4

Reflection Questions

What Scriptures bring you peace in the time of grief, chaos and confusion?

On the Other Side of Through

Angie Green

As I Grieved

Angie Green

On the Other Side of Through

He Needed His Wife

When we stated our vows, we had no idea that "To death do us part" included our children. The tragic losses affected our marriage: emotionally, relationally and spiritually.

Per Jean Galica, a licensed marriage and family therapist, "The death of a child usually acts to polarize the existing factors found in the marriage; hence, some marriages get worse, some get better, some just maintain and some end in divorce."[2]

The death of a child violates the natural order of life. We expect to raise children and watch them grow to adulthood. We expect to create memories with them. We expect our children to bury us, not the other way around.

In the beginning, Jonathan and I comforted one another. But as time progressed, and my grief engulfed me, Jonathan's compassion shifted to worry. He worried about me; he worried about our children and I neglected to be there for him.

We had been ripped apart. We didn't have anything left to offer each other. I could not comfort

---

[2]Source: *The Effects of the Death of a Child on a Marriage,* online: www.theravive.com/research/the-effects-of-the-death-of-a-child-on-a-marriage (accessed February 5, 2018).

him because I was empty of everything, but pain, confusion and anger.

Although we didn't argue, the silence between us was deafening. We distanced ourselves from each other; withdrew to opposing corners of life's boxing ring. Jonathan's over-the-road driving already had him gone weeks at a time, so we easily fell into isolation. That suited me because I wasn't obligated to attend to his needs. The frequency of our phone calls remained the same, but our conversations were different.

Distance, isolation and lack of communication affected intimacy. We had allowed the stealth serpent to deceive us with subtle lies. Once we realized that the enemy was trying to sabotage our relationship, we recommitted our love and sought God. Our relationship improved, and Jonathan put his family first by leaving his job to be home with us.

Despite our individual struggles, I thank God that we didn't blame each other. We agreed that we were great parents to JóNiah. We acknowledged that we loved her in unique ways. We committed to pray for—and with—each other.

Our dynamics are different without JóNiah, but we work hard, as a unit, to honor our relationship. We grieve together. We help each other through hard times. We don't go it alone because we know we have each other. We keep the lines of communication open between us and our children. We vowed to be there for each other, no matter what problems we faced, and we do just that.

I pray for my husband daily.

> "Lord, give Jonathan Your peace. Let him understand Your sovereign will. Let him dwell in Your secret place. Comfort him. Father, I ask that You help me to reverence my husband. Thank You for showing us Your unconditional love as a model for marriage. Thank You for keeping us as a threefold cord that's not easily broken. I ask for Your divine protection over my family. In the matchless name of Your Son, in the name of Jesus, amen."

My husband is my rock. When I have meltdowns, he consoles me. He reminds me that things will be okay and that we'll get through this…together.

Angie Green

On the Other Side of Through

They Needed Their Mother

Telling Raven and Justin that they would never see their sister again amplified the horrific experience ten times.

Jon and I left the emergency room where our baby had been pronounced dead. We walked to the waiting room where family and friends had gathered.

Raven, who was home from college on summer break, cried uncontrollably when she learned that her sister had drowned.

Because Justin was seven years old and not capable of comprehending death, he had more difficulty understanding. He had so many questions.

"Why can't I see my sister?"

"Because when a person dies we have to bury them."

"How can I call her?"

"You can't call her on the phone, but she's watching over you from heaven. She's your guardian angel."

Answering Justin's questions drained me because I didn't believe the words that were coming out of my mouth.

I held my children as tight as I could as they wept: for their sister, for each other, for themselves.

Smotherly Motherly Love

I didn't want my children to experience the aftermath of this tsunami. The torrential rains, gale-force winds and massive flooding made me overprotective. I tried to keep them in arms' reach; I held them hostage.

When the time came for Raven to return to her dorm, I didn't want her to leave. Having my children near me was the only way to verify their safety.

When I realized that my crippling fear was smothering the life out of them, I asked God to help me. I didn't want to feel vulnerable. I had to release the anxiety that they were in harm's way when I couldn't see them. I didn't want my children to resent me. I needed Him to ease my mind.

Another aspect of my smotherly love was not allowing Raven and Justin to see me upset. While Jon and I tried to maintain some sense of normalcy, I didn't want to add to their worry.

Dr. Chris Overtree, a child and family psychologist, said, "Parents are generally inclined to pretend everything is fine. But kids are way more hip to our feelings than we think. 'When we try to hide our grief, we're not that successful at doing it and it usually comes out in other ways.'"³

I had to get my grief under subjection to help my children through theirs. As the flight attendant states before takeoff, "In the event of a sudden loss of cabin pressure, oxygen masks will drop from the overhead compartment. Put on your mask first and then help others."

Raven and Justin grieve differently. For two years, Justin went into JóNiah's room to touch her things. He said that it made him feel close to her especially since we left it untouched for three years.

Jon and I sure they knew that they can talk to us any time and we encourage them to express their feelings. On occasion, we gather at the dining room table to reminisce about JóNiah. We let them laugh in a guilt-free, no-judgement environment.

Grief Counseling for My Children

At one point, Justin withdrew. Fear of abandonment kept him from associating with other children. Because I was immersed in grief and knew that I was not a parenting expert, I sought help for my children. After extensive online research, I hired

---

³ Source: *Parenting While Heartbroken: The Dos and Don'ts*, online: www.rachelsimmons.com/parenting-while-heartbroken-the-dos-and-donts (accessed September 24, 2017).

professionals to explain to them that their feelings were valid, normal and okay.

My children and I attended grief counseling for a year. We talked about our catastrophic tidal wave with others dealing with similar issues. The interaction helped them.

After counseling, Justin expressed his feelings more freely. He reopened his heart and became more outgoing. He's doing quite well and has tons of friends.

Parents must realize that children grieve and need help to process their emotions for healthier grieving. Getting professional help for your children is beneficial for them and you.

Many resources are available to help children process grief including counseling agencies that operate by grants and contributions. These organizations provide free services. See the *Resources for Grief* on page 85.

On the Other Side of Through

What Not to Say to a Grieving Person

Oftentimes, people don't know what to say in times of loss. Some people tend to regurgitate tired platitudes they feel are appropriate and soothing. But for me, they were quite the opposite.

I grew tired of the sympathetic clichés and remained silent, so as not to offend the person trying to comfort me. However, in my mind, I wanted them to shut up and leave me alone.

The following thoughtless condolences angered, irritated and upset me:

"You must be special to God since He chose you like He chose Job."

"The Lord needed an angel."

"The Lord won't put more on you than you can bear."

"She's in a better place."

"You didn't know this was going to happen."

"You couldn't control what happened to her."

"At least you had her for eight years."

"Better to have loved and loss, then never to have loved at all."

And the most-upsetting condolence: "God knows best."

Although many of the sayings are Bible-based, they may not be well-received, especially if the griever has not fully processed the situation. I was not trying to hear anything about God or what He wanted. I wanted my daughter back.

Since loss is inevitable, consider encouraging someone by
- Giving them time and space to grieve
- Mailing inspirational greeting cards to their home two or more weeks after the funeral service
- Expressing sentiments like
    - "You're in my thoughts and prayers."
    - "Here's my number. Call whenever you need to talk."

Reflection Questions

What words of encouragement would you share with someone who's grieving?

_____

_____

_____

In Memory of JóNiah

To honor JóNiah's memory, Jonathan and I created the JóNiah B. Green Scholarship. We have awarded two scholarships and plan to annually honor young ladies who love to dance.

We also created *Niah B* Lip Gloss as part of a makeup line by JóNiah's Aunt Liz. The gloss is nude with a little sparkle; like JóNiah loved. When I wear the gloss, I feel like she's with me.

JóNiah brought us tremendous joy the eight years we had her. Letting her go has been difficult, but we are at a place where we focus on the wonderful memories we created together. When we miss her, we watch videos. A year after she died, we found videos she had made on her father's tablet. I believe it was her way of telling us that she's okay and to remind us to cherish her memories.

Angie Green

Resources for Grief

Jennifer J. Matthews, PhD, LPC, NCC, ACS
Hope and Restoration Counseling
29623 Northwestern Hwy #5
Southfield, MI 48034
248.462.6857
HopeAndRestorationCounseling.com
Individual counseling and free grief support group

Sandcastles
1 Ford Place
Detroit, MI 48202
313.874.6881
AboutSandCastles.org
Grief support program for children ages 3-18 and their families

Ele's Place
ElesPlace.org
Michigan-based healing center for children and teens

Online Resources

CompassionateFriends.org provides grief support after the death of a child.

GloryBabies.com is a Christ-centered support group offering hope and healing for those grieving the loss of a baby during pregnancy or infancy and/or struggling with infertility.

JourneyOfHearts.org is an online healing place for anyone grieving loss.

MyGriefAngels.org/Grief-Support-Directory-.html lists grief support services by type of loss.

OpenToHope.com gives a voice to grief and recovery, and helps people find hope after loss.

Want to Experience More?

You are invited to join the *On the Other Side of Through: Life After Loss* Facebook community to connect with others on the path to reclaiming their lives after the death of their children.

To order books in bulk; inquire about speaking availability, program offerings and book signings, visit **AngieSpeaks.net** or email AngieSpeaks.net@gmail.com.

Angie Green

About Angie Green

After the deaths of four children, Angie Green felt rejected, abandoned, forgotten. Consumed with grief, overwhelmed with anger and convinced that God was punishing her, she lost faith, trust and hope in Him.

As the anger turned inward, depression stifled her. She struggled to get out of bed, resisted daily routines and yearned for the past. This tumultuous whirlwind spun her out of control for almost four years before she realized that God was not trying to kill her, but rather build her for ministry.

In *On the Other Side of Through: Life After Loss*, Green shares how the joys of parenthood were snatched by guilt and grief, until she let go and let God.

When others run from the storms of life, Green treks forward to prove that life after loss is achievable with Christ.

For speaking engagements, bookings and other information, visit **AngieSpeaks.net**.

Angie Green

About Queen V Publishing

The Doorway to YOUR Destiny!

Go thou and publish abroad the kingdom of God.
— Luke 9:60 ESV

Committed to transforming manuscripts into polished works of art, **Queen V Publishing** is a company of standard and integrity. We offer an alternative that allows the message in YOU to do what it was sent to do for OTHERS.

QueenVPublishing.com

Serving professional speakers and experts to magnify and monetize their message by publishing quality books

Angie Green

On the Other Side of Through

To order additional copies of
On the Other Side of Through
18726 Schoolcraft Road
Detroit, MI 48223
AngieSpeaks.net
313.397.7029

* * * * * * * * * * * * * * * * * *

_____
Name

_____
Address

_____
City / State / Zip

(_____)_____
Phone

_____
Email

Quantity	Price Per Book	Total
	$11.95	
Sales Tax (MI residents add $0.72 per book)		
Shipping ($2.99 first book, $0.99 each add'l)		
Grand Total* (Payable to: Angie Green)		

* Certified check and money orders only

Available on Amazon.com in paperback and Kindle!

Angie Green

www.ingramcontent.com/pod-product-compliance
Lightning Source LLC
Chambersburg PA
CBHW050442010526
44118CB00013B/1641